THE SELECTED POEMS OF GWENDOLEN HASTE

Ahsahta Press

Boise State University
Boise, Idaho

Versions of some of the poems contained in this volume have appeared in **Young Land** and in various periodicals from 1922 to 1959; "Dialog" and "Legend" were provided by the Billings, Montana, Public Library.

Copyright © 1976 by Gwendolen Haste

ISBN 0-916272-01-X

Library of Congress Catalog Card Number
75-29916

Contents

Preface

I. The New Land

In A New Land	13
Montana Wives:	14
The Ranch In The Coulee	14
The Old Farm Wife	15
The Wind	16
Vengeance	17
Deliverance	18
The Stoic	19
Horizons	20
Dried Out	21
For A Lonely Grave	22
Exotic	23
The Little Theatre	24
Nostalgia	25
The Reason	26
Prairie Wolf	27
Cumae	28
Winter Homecoming	29
Borgia	30
Vanished	32
The Solitary	33
The Mocker	34
The Outlander's Wife	35
He's Taken Her Back Again	36
Ophidia	37
Outcast	38
The Horseman	39
Prayer Of The Homesteader	40

II. Later Poems

After Appomattox	45
Dialog	47
Legend	48

Bedroom	49
Death Of The Grandmother	50
Tomorrow Is A Birthday	53
The Return	54
Revisit I: Peace At Midnight	55
Revisit IV: Words On Departure	56
Transcontinental	57
Dorchester Plate	59
Language Of Pain	60
Over Patras	61

Note:
Poems are dated in italics to indicate probable date of composition, in medium type to indicate date of first publication.

Preface

Even though Gwendolen Haste has lived and worked in New York City since 1925, she is still a Western poet. She spent a number of her most productive years in Billings, Montana, helping her father edit the **Scientific Farmer**; and her best poems picture the lives of ranchers—men, women, and children—in the years when the West was being settled. She was born December 4, 1889, in Streator, Illinois, and grew up in Wisconsin; after graduating from the University of Chicago in 1912, she worked with her father first in Lincoln, Nebraska, later in Billings. Except for the year 1918 in the East as a munitions worker during World War I, she remained in Billings from 1915 to 1925. In the mid-twenties Ms. Haste moved East permanently, first to join the editorial staff of **Survey** magazine and later to work with the Consumer Service Department of General Foods Corporation. She was secretary of the Poetry Society of America from 1928-29 and remained on its board of directors until 1935. In 1936 she was married to Marlin Douglass Hennesey of Hillsboro, N.H. In 1955-1956, she served as secretary of the Westerners, a group of writers, artists, librarians, publishers representatives, and hobbyists with western and historical interests.

Her poems were published in numerous national magazines; one titled "The Ranch in the Coulee" shared **The Nation** poetry prize in 1922. Her one volume of poetry, **Young Land** (Coward-McCann, 1930), contains the series "Montana Wives," which includes some of her most vivid and precise works, calling up the bleak, wind-swept landscapes of the barren Montana rangeland, and the bleak and barren—TV and movies notwithstanding—lives of many who lived there.

These Western poems still—forty and more years later—speak strongly of and to the experience of women anywhere—on a ranch, in a suburb, in a city. Perhaps this is because they speak of a loneliness, an isolation, a boredom that is localized in the poems, and yet universal. Many of Ms. Haste's readers have noted this universality and immediacy in the poems; for example, a New England housewife wrote her to say "That woman might have been myself" of the Montana wife in "The Ranch in the Coulee" who goes mad, hemmed in by her limited horizon and opportunities.

Certainly it is this ability to combine a strong local flavor with universal human feeling that makes Ms. Haste such an original figure in her own day and such a remarkable one in ours. As with so many poems written by women, and lost, forgotten, or ignored after an initial success, we are apt to see them today and say, "When was this written?" Her feelings about women are "right" and her details of the West are right: the June river running at full flood, the play of sun on a single cottonwood, the feeling of anticipation as one comes toward the crest of a hill on a dusty back road, "What's ahead?"

As Ms. Haste's poetry shows no danger of succumbing to the illusions of the feminine mystique, so too it rejects the stereotypes of all those rugged, hearty, and hardy ranch wives, hands raised over suntanned brows as they gaze courageously westward, the indomitable spirits. Surely, Ms. Haste's depiction of ranch women is at least as close to reality as the sanitized, commercialized version, for between moments when the indomitable spirit was operating, there must have been long hours when "one by one her little hopes had fled/ Down through those racking, windy, drouth-filled years." "The Stoic" is certainly a memorial to both sides of the ranch woman's life, her pride and her endurance, as well as her suffering and her despair. Along with "The Stoic," where the vision is grim but not hopeless, there are poems about those who cannot endure, who break under the strain, losing their sanity, like the wife in "Ranch in the Coulee," or the woman in "Exotic," who has grown sour, bitter, her soul "withered like last year's weeds."

Ms. Haste expresses much of the same bleakness, the same loneliness, the same deadening effect of endless drudgery as does her contemporary Willa Cather in her novels and short stories of Middle Western farm life. The sonnet "Nostalgia," for example, recalls both in subject and in tone Cather's "A Wagner Matinee." And the desperate weariness of the wife in "The Reason" is reminiscent of Susan Glaspell's short story "A Jury of Her Peer" (1917), in which more contented wives understand and protect one whose loneliness and desperation has driven her to murder.

Still, though most strongly aware of the difficulties of ranch life, occasionally Ms. Haste's work suggests its beauties, there for those who can see them. Alas, in "Vengeance," the efficient farm wife sees nothing of the beauty and drama of the sunrise, the storm clouds over the mountains, the virginal dance of a single cottonwood tree. One wonders, indeed, if Ms. Haste's ranch women survive best in being least sensitive—to both beauty and barrenness.

Ms. Haste seems to have produced her best work under the control of rhyme and meter; and for the most part her best poems are her Western ones. In them she seems most in touch with the land and with people. Some of her later "Eastern" poems tend to abstraction and lack of focus, though they still contain the occasional striking image.

Still, whatever the shortcomings of some of her late works, her best is of excellent quality, the reflections of a woman, not herself a ranch wife, but one entirely in touch with the feelings and experiences of women everywhere, especially women of the West.

Carol Mullaney
Boise State University
March 1, 1976

I. The New Land

In A New Land

It stands forlorn
Under dying trees
Among little houses all bright with paint
Where hopes are fresh
And children young
Where years and living have left no taint.

Those who built it
Died long ago
When that cottonwood tree was tender in leaf.
They came and went
But they left their ghosts,
Old ghosts from lands that are dark with grief.

These little houses
Just learning life
Will their porches sag and their lawns grow thin?
Will spirits crowd
In their dusty rooms
To cry old sorrow and mourn old sin?

1924

Montana Wives

The Ranch In The Coulee

He built the ranch house down a little draw,
So that he should have wood and water near.
The bluffs rose all around. She never saw
The arching sky, the mountains lifting clear;
But to the west the close hills fell away
And she could glimpse a few feet of the road.
The stage to Roundup went by every day,
Sometimes a rancher town-bound with his load,
An auto swirling dusty through the heat,
Or children trudging home on tired feet.

At first she watched it as she did her work,
A horseman pounding by gave her a thrill,
But then within her brain began to lurk
The fear that if she lingered from the sill
Someone might pass unseen. So she began
To keep the highroad always within sight,
And when she found it empty long she ran
And beat upon the pane and cried with fright.
The winter was the worst. When snow would fall
He found it hard to quiet her at all.

1922

The Old Farm Wife

Grin toothlessly up at the sun
  Spring's begun.
Winter wheat, now snow is gone
  Coming on;
And the plow has cut each field
  Quick to yield
Rippling harvest, tall and mellow,
  Green and yellow.
Now what difference make the years
  Grey with tears,
Or the body marred with toil
  On the soil?
What is age and what is pain
  When the rain
Peacefully blots out the sun
  With plowing done.

1922

The Wind

The cabin sits alone far up a hill
Where all the year the mournful wind blows shrill.

She used to tell him sometimes: "No one knows
How hard it is to listen while it blows."

He never touched a plow again, they say,
After he found her there, but went away.

And tenants wouldn't live upon the place
Because, the neighbors said, they saw her face

Pressed close against the little window-pane
Watching the twisting storm clouds in the rain,

And in the night time they could hear her cry
And moan and whimper if the gale was high.

So now through barren fields the great winds blow
Where fan weed and the purple wild pea grow.

They said she had no cause to die, but still
The wind was always blowing on that hill.

1922

Vengeance

The sun came up with a nice display
   Of amber and rose;
   And at end of day
There was orange or crimson or amethyst
   Whichever you chose.
   But she never saw.
The storms hurried up from behind the mountains
   And spread great clouds
   Like boiling fountains
And covered the fresh blue sky with shrouds.
   She only said "Pshaw!"
And went out to gather the clothes from the line.
Then the cottonwood tree in the yard
Danced like a virgin before a shrine.
   She looked at it hard
And said "Cottonwood trees are so messy."
   At last she died
And was buried in black, very dressy.
   Her relations cried;
But the sunset poured out scarlet and blue,
   Purple and gold;
While the cottonwood danced the whole day through
   When they put her away to mould.

1922

Deliverance

The screaming kingbirds in the poplars woke her,
And since lately there had been no joy in waking,
She thought it well to end such things, together
With floors to scrub and baking.

So instead of lifting up the pails, she turned
Down to the river rushing brown in flood
And watched a moment the June sunlight sifting
Through a lone cottonwood.

An easy way it was to end all wakings,
To hear no more the flooded river's strife,
Nor noisy birds at dawn, nor cows at milk-time,
Nor any voice of life.

1922

The Stoic

She guessed there wasn't any time for tears
Because her heart had held them all unshed
While one by one her little hopes had fled
Down through those racking, windy, drouth-
 filled years.
The frozen winter when the cattle died,
The year the hail bent flat the tender wheat,
The thirsty summers with their blazing heat—
She met them all with wordless, rigid pride.

But when, sometimes, the children in the spring
Searching through barren hill or ragged butte,
Would heap her lap with loco blooms, and bring
Clouds of blue larkspur and bright bitter-root,
Then would she run away to hide her pain
For memory of old gardens drenched with rain.

1921

Horizons

I had to laugh,
For when she said it we were sitting by the door,
And straight down was the Fork,
Twisting and turning and gleaming in the sun.
And then your eyes carried across to the purple
 bench beyond the river
With the Beartooth Mountains fairly screaming
 with light and blue and snow,
And fold and turn of rimrock and prairie as far
 as your eye could go.

And she says: "Dear Laura, sometimes I feel so
 sorry for you,
Shut away from everything—eating out your
 heart with loneliness.
When I think of my own full life I wish that you
 could share it.
Just pray for happier days to come and bear it."

She goes back to Billings to her white stucco
 house,
And looks through net curtains at another white
 stucco house,
And a brick house,
And a yellow frame house,
And six trimmed poplar trees,
And little squares of shaved grass.

Oh dear, she stared at me like I was daft!
I couldn't help it. I just laughed and laughed!

1922

Dried Out

This place was the first home we ever had,
And I was sick of farming for other folks—
First in Wisconsin and then in Dakota.
It looked so pretty when he broke sod that day.
There wa'n't only three sides to the house,
But what did I care!
There was sunlight and wet rain and a coulee
    full of springtime where the children could
    play.

Seven full years, says the Book, and seven lean—
And we come in at the end of the full ones, I
    guess.
There ain't no crops where they's no rain.
And the stock died in the big blizzard.
So now we're goin'
Back to Dakota to farm for other folks.

Oh God, the nice white ranch house with a floor
We was to have! The roses by the door!

1922

For A Lonely Grave

The wind cannot hurt
As it beats on her ears—
They are stopped with dirt.
And her heart is still
So it cannot leap
At the wail of the wolf
From the top of the hill.
She will never weep
As she lies alone.
Her nights will be quiet
Beneath this stone.

1922

Exotic

Her frightened soul shrank
When she saw
The bitter crumbling hills of shale.
And the high cutbank,
Gashed and raw,
Struck her eyes like the wall of a jail.

The years ran by
Indifferent
And she never grew used to unfenced land,
Nor dust blown high,
Nor scrub pines bent
In the midst of shuffling wastes of sand.

When she was old
Her voice was sour
And her eyes were as hard as small black beads.
Her mouth was cold
And twisted and dour
For her soul had withered like last year's weeds.

1922

The Little Theatre

They coaxed him from his barren lonely claim
And taught him how to stride across the stage,
And how to whisper love, and how to rage,
And how to smile in treachery's cold game.
He felt the mounting glory of his fame
When in the simple eyes beyond the beam
Of lanterns he could see the answering gleam
Of that which in his soul was living flame.

Now though the hail has stripped his acres bare
He watches but the gold of Rosalind's hair.
The prairie can be withered by the drouth
He only yearns for Juliet's young mouth;
And while the blizzard hammers at his door
He's locked with life and fate at Elsinore.

1922

Nostalgia

He brought the record home with sheepish pride
And wound the old machine. The crystal notes
Swirled through the little room like gleaming motes
In jeweled light. He listened open-eyed;
But when she wept he tiptoed from her side,
His own eyes dim for cherry blooms and tears,
The crimson rapture, the unspoken fears,
The lyric sorrow of the wistful bride.

He could not know her grief was not for pain
Of love forsaken, but that far away
Were scented beauty piled in galleries,
Wealth, color, silver voices, proud display—
While here stretched out the long and dusty plain
With great buttes shouldering the windy skies.

1923

The Reason

She told them when they came and found him there
That he had tried to kill her with the knife—
Although she knew that he would never dare
To threaten her—much less to take her life.
So they who had seen his rages let her go.
But brooding on it in the later years
She felt she might have stood each curse and blow,
His shouting anger or his brutal jeers,
But on that day her heart was tired and sore
With God's austere and high indifference.
She saw the withered fields beyond the door,
The rotting barns, the filth, the broken fence,
And all her faded days, robbed of delight,
Where everything but weariness had fled,
So when he came in lowering that night
She took the rabbit gun and shot him dead.

1924

Prairie Wolf

North of the house there was a graveled range of hills,
Stubborn and bare with clinging grey dry grass,
Where, resting sometimes through her vacant days, she watched
The far swift shadows of the coyotes pass.

She told herself her life was like those stony hills,
Unfertile, bitter in the blaze of noon,
Where fearful yellow shapes slipped by uncertainly
And wailed for sorrow underneath the moon.

1924

Cumae

Right from the very first I felt that fate
Was hanging round the place.
It wasn't the fling above us of the butte
That made it queer.
I've lived in wilder places and more desolate
And had no fear.
But nothing I could do would lift the strangeness from the shack.
I made white curtains, planted flowers,
And had a garden out in back.
I even tried to get a tree to grow!
Four walls, two windows and a floor—
You wouldn't think it spooky just to see.
But I could hardly bear to close the door—
Looking and waiting—for what I didn't know.

But that grey morning when I missed him from the bed
And went out searching round the house
And found him in the shed,
His toes just off the floor—swing—swinging—
And I flew
Those three rough miles to town
My throat torn with a scream,
Why then—I knew!
I knew!

1925

Winter Homecoming

The white night of the winter stretches wide.
The black night of the winter presses low.
Outside the open barn door stands the team
With chilly breath rising above the snow.

The yellow lantern throws a little light
Upon them and the open swinging door,
A man and woman slow and dumb with cold,
A winter-barren tree and nothing more.

The stars are worlds of flame but they are far,
Pricking the blackness of the bitter night.
They cannot warm these winter-frozen ones
Within that wavering circle of pale light.

1926

Borgia

From one end of the valley to the other
You still hear word of them.
Although some secret startling death
Has snatched them all, brother and brother,
Long years away from that grey ranch house by the river,
Yet they exist in tales.

Not tales that have a right to cling
To this young land,
Of wolves and shooting irons and gambling,
Of men ruthless as savages and young as gods;
But troubling tales,
Strange as those told of venomous princes
In plotting capitals of desperate states,
Tales threaded through with jeweled poisonous fates.
Tales that are honey-colored by mad sins.

What was their heritage?
What horrid stains
Came with them in their journey through the plains
To soil their turbulent blood?
Nobody knows.
The stories only tell of this hot rage
Of life begun in cruelty and woes
Ending in scarlet violence and the grave.

Yet the house stands beside the noisy stream,
A little hidden by grey cottonwoods,
Peacefully vacant—smiling in its dream;
The house where one was born whose life snapped out
Among perfumes and sandalwood and spring;
The home in childhood of that twisted soul
Whose deeds are whispered by the shattered coal,
Scarce understood by those whose slow lives rust
In sheep and marketing,
And careful lust.

There was a garden here,
So long ago.
Somebody planted lilac trees and phlox.
These hollyhocks
Trembled when one was driven out to die,
Raving among the heedless empty hills,
So that blanched sheep herders still hear his cry.

The wind quivers among the cottonwoods
And draws a pleasant murmur from that pine.
Is there no taint where the mild sunlight spills?
No drifting murk along these hovering hills?
No sign?

1926

Vanished

Why did she go,
Quickly between morning and twilight,
Making no sign,
Leaving the wash beating the line,
The lettuce ungathered?
Was it because the mountains were suddenly too bare,
Lying like gray wrinkled elephants along the sky?
Or did she tire of the wheat field's yellow stare?
Or was it because that night
The wind rose
And fled through the hills with a singing cry?

1926

The Solitary

Whenever she's in town she leaves the shops
And wanders off to beauty on a street
Shaded by pleasant trees, where bungalows
Are white and green, where clover lawns are neat,
Where zinnias and bright nasturtiums bloom.
Each house is built close to another one
So women every afternoon can sit
Upon the porches when their work is done,
And talk to other women and crochet.
Autos rush by. A cheerful phonograph
Sends sudden music, while across the lawns
A group of noisy children play and laugh.

Then she goes back and climbs into the Ford
To ride long miles out where there is no sound
Except the wind, a rooster's crow, the hens,
The eternal crickets singing from the ground,
And past the further hillside a faint smoke—
All that she sees of any other folk.

1926

The Mocker

The cowboy comes to town
Scornful.
He wears his orange wool chaps
And scarlet handkerchief,
And embroidered boots;
Under him is his beautiful silver-mounted
 saddle.
He meets his friends down by the tracks
In a huddle of old buildings
That were there before the railroad.
But sometimes he rides his pony out on Spencer
 Avenue.
He digs his spurs in the pony's side,
And the pony bucks,
And the cowboy whoops most insolent and con-
 temptuous
Outside the fine brick residence of the President
 of the First State Bank.
Almost the cowboy would urge his pony over the
 brick coping among the shrubbery and
 perennials
But that sacrilege is forbidden—
Even to cowboys.

1927

The Outlander's Wife

She married young
A man from down the river
With odd and twisted ways—
Not ours—
And foreign tongue.
Her children gabble like young jays.
Her house is strange.
Her very pigs and chickens queer.
She has to spend her wifely days
Learning to cook
Unfriendly dishes.
She has a look
That seems to say
I do not understand.
Why am I here?
How have I strayed,
To what far desperate land?

1927

He's Taken Her Back Again

She has come back,
And we peer behind the curtains,
And whisper in the store.
She has come back
And has washed her curtains,
And is buying flour and butter at the store.
She has wistful hazel eyes,
And a crooked smile.
Now she irons, sweeps and fries,
And hangs out clothes on Monday.
For marriage time is reckoned from Sunday to Sunday,
And for her who has returned
It is all one day;
With curtains between her and a time that is dead,
And trips to the store for a loaf of bread.

1927

Ophidia

Lifting dark beside the trail,
Blotched by the pale
Sunlight sifting down cedars;
Mark of beast—stir of bee—
But here no least foot of man has beaten track,
And the traveler shudders back
From the narrow needled floor.
This is a door into legend,
Tales of men caught among patterned horror,
Before caverns painted with sun,
With clubbed gun a slack weapon
Rasping a last breath
In swollen death.

Let the mild cedars roar
Over the cushioned floor
While the tales pour
Down the wind from that place of bright caverns,
Down paths known only to wild feet and the dead—
The dread touch of life that lies in the sunlight alone,
Warm on a stone.

1929

Outcast

Old man Carver
Came from the East.
He never sat
At their thundering feast.

He never knew
Their whiskeyed nights.
He was farming stones
While they hunted fights.

When they told of bloody
Barroom rows,
Carver could only
Speak of cows.

His words of seed corn
Were nothing beside
The story of Jed
And the grey wolf's hide.

So he sat dumb
In the crossroad store
While they spun shattering
Tales of gore.

They granted Carver
Could farm like hell,
But he had no beautiful
Lies to tell.

1930

The Horseman

Dust on the trail—then a blot—
Somebody coming. It's not
Usual here in this spot
Off the main highway—forgot
By the world. But he's nearer. He rides
At a trot on the level. He hides
Where the shoulder of sandstone obscures
The white cloud of his passing. He lures
Our eyes from the harrow and churn.
We taste of his coming. We yearn
For his voice, for the word of the trail,
For the pipefuls, the leisurely hail
And farewell of the dwellers alone
On the skirts of the high peaks of stone.
One more turn and he'll be at the door.
Quick, catch up the pail from the floor,
His horse will be thirsty, and set
The bench in the shadow, and get
Some food on the stove. "Step right down;
Take a seat. What's the good news from town?"
But he answers us shortly—a drink
For his horse from the spring—do we think
He can make Canyon City by dark?
We point out a blue ridge to mark.
He is cold and apart from our words.
He looks over the mountains—the birds
Are not more incurious. He shakes
The reins; the horse moves; silence breaks
On the hills, the thin trail, the tilled field.
He is gone. He will nevermore yield
Cheerful secrets of where he has been,
What has done, what has said, what has seen,
His name and his station—his flight
Has gathered them all. In the light
We watch him ascending the height,
More strange than the mountains and night.

1930

Prayer of the Homesteader

Dear Lord, we are afraid.
We do not know this land.
These mountains are too cold and tall and bare.
Within their flanks the grey wolf has his lair.
Safety lay thick upon the fields
And friendly hilltops of our youth.
Lord, you will understand
We are not cowards
But we do not like this land.

We were taught simple things when we were young.
We know the path a plow makes in black loam,
The way of pleasant showers on April days,
The soft winds of our home.
We know the healing rains of summer nights,
And the gold plenty of the harvesting.
But this land fights.
Its hard brown sod protests against the plow,
Its stubborn grasses cling.
Our young crops are beat flat by roaring hail,
And when the rains should visit us in spring
There comes a hot strange gale,
Like desert wind blown over glittering sand
That dries the little wheat.
Lord, did you mean that men should farm this land?

Lord, this is not a land where men should live.
Our minds rake up a harvest of old tales
Whispered around old fires,
And butte and coulee ring with chattering wails.
Upon these iron benches Things have stalked.
When morning breaks we are afraid to look
For fear great feet have walked
And left crushed tracks upon the buffalo grass.
These creeping nights of ghosts were never made
For man and sleep.
Dear Lord, we are afraid.

Lord, can it be that this is not your land?
Your ways are peaceful ways through country lanes,
But you have never walked upon these plains,
We never see your face beneath these skies.
Come to us, Lord.
Man should not live alone within the world;
He is not strong nor wise.
Bless our thin crops.
Teach the small trees to grow.
Stretch us your kindly hand.
We must have comfort in this alien land.

1922

II. Later Poems

After Appomattox

Let there be heavier fruit large among leaves,
A golden heaping of sun on earth.
This will be a year of reaping,
When the warm body soft under leaf shadow
Will tremble beneath urging hands.
Let no cloud hide this fire of summer.

Forget that which has been lived
And was called girlhood.
Girl days should flutter with hidden loves—
Happiness of early arbutus and birds among the evening trees.
That which is over
Has been terrible with enduring,
Loverless, noisy with the names of the dead.
Thrust the years of drouth away.
Remember only childhood with apples and sunlight.
Tears are not good to remember.

Girlhood lived with death;
But now there is no death,
Only the sweet wild plum ripening,
The corn tasseling in the steamy heat.
Now there is a seeping into the land,
A return of that which has been gone.
There will be thin leaping men in farmhouses,
Voices that burn.
No longer the blurred notes of old men nor the clatter of women.
There will be shouts and whistling in the fields.

It is a summer for ripeness.
Put aside the close dress,
Smooth the hid ribbon.
This is a summer for glancing and laughter.
Remember the ways of dancing,
The words of bright songs.
Quicken your tongue to answer.
There will be questions.

It is for this that the live breast pulls the bodice,
For this flesh is cool and honey-pale.
Take the flecked sun on cheek and lip—
A woman is passive before the intruder.
Listen for a foot on the roadway,
A voice at the wide door.

1933

Dialog

The cold flows thickly round the house. It turns
The hills to brittle shards. There is no soul
In our warmth or the fire's that speaks in words
It knows. I hate its cruelty and disregard.

    Within the bed those furnaces our bodies
    Lie consuming life. We plot to burn
    An ever-leaping fire. What difference
    to us the cold learns nothing of it?

This land is like a bride, fleshless and wild,
But never fat with child. It has two virtues,
Beauty and pride, but to a woman these
Are neither virtues. Yet you seem to love it.

    The living seize each other on the plains.
    I find my breath struggling with the cattle,
    Beating through blizzard to the feeding pens,
    And with the rains I yearn over the wheat.

Rains and the spring are far. They hardly smooth
The thing I mean. You buy yourself
With crops and calving, but that face uncouth
Behind the wheat is what you've never seen.

    The wind has changed while we've been talking. Hear
    That friend of ranches in the winter humming
    Above our roof. The cold is gone. The eaves
    Will smoke with comfort after the sunrise.

Oh, little man, impressed with kindliness,
There is no heart in that wind's dripping cheer!
This land is ruthless as the universe.
The circling stars cannot be more malign
Than these flat plains and fearful peaks and skies.

1938

Legend

The summer breeze drove Madoc gently west.
His bitter sailors clung about the stern
Seeing the crest of Wales turn into cloud.
The blind, infernal water shone below.
Madoc, scatheless of devils, hunted peace.

On that sad coast where the keel hung at last
Forest and prairie fell behind his feet,
Until, above a tumbling curve of green,
The Shining Mountains broke upon the sky.

"Here will be peace," said Madoc.
Where the high streams feed the Missouri
Madoc's men stretched roofs and raised their sons.
The moccasin stopped at the breath of Wales
Clashing among the cedars.

Gazing at snow, plucking the mountain lily,
Madoc rolled peace upon his tongue
    till death.

1939

Bedroom

This is the place where living does not come,
Where the equipment of the day is never brought.
Neatness may have its way here.   This high room
Will stand reminding us what sun has taught—
The best of life may still be sleep.   Draw
The pale sheet over the solemn rectangle,
See that the curtains keep the window's law.
Let nothing be askew or dangle.
So that one coming in from the distress
Of day will watch receding the last beams
Of living; with but one duty, to undress,
And cope with the faint necessities of dreams.

1940

Death of the Grandmother

It is almost forgotten . . . the stepping down from swinging
    light
To the night crossed by the shape of trees; grumble of
    motion
And the smell of horses, dull penumbras of light and tall
    blackness.
There is no home in these streets, only recollections of odor,
    light,
Motion, from days when things broke in the mind to foam-
    ing outlines.
Far back in the sleepy brain a faintly known remembering
Swings with the creak of the omnibus and iron shoes on
    brick pavement.

This is a return through saved memories to the slippered
    scuffle.
Long since the large grace of the Persian lilac was old with
    the grapevine
Bending on its trellis. Ponies that once stamped in the barn
Died long ago; ridden no more by girls now lost in taffeta
And emerald-glinting hands, passing the frail cup,
Tipping the brass shine above the spirit lamp.
Go back . . . renew yourself in these colored wells.

Lamps shed paleness spilling on dark cupboards, painted
    glass doors
Holding all that has gone. The catalpas have dropped green
    pencils
Now dry-patterned brown on cold lawn. Nothing is left of
    the peonies
But a round death. As sleep curtains the mind there are
    bells,
Minor clangings that fall through the catalpa boughs . . .
The whistle at crossing . . . the muffled voice of the
    shunting . . .
Dreams in this strange yet remembered house circled by
    bells.

For the young the old die with ease, a ceasing in quiet of one
Who was kind hands. Too early to learn death. The habit
Of funeral strikes queerly . . . a loss not felt but remem-
 bered in pictures
Crude with infancy, before that face had changed to the
 remote glance
From the sheet or the voice was stilled by the death-coming.
 Pictures that lie
In the remembering mind while the eyes watch an old man
 lost in deafness
And grief who speaks of a past known only to the blood not
 the memory.

April, and nothing will hinder the catalpa from urging her
 rich blossom,
Nor will the blue grape ever cease, and the locust
Over the herringbone drive has an eternity with the house.
Only years will mix shingles and graceful dish, the catalpa
 and the clap of hooves
And the sad harmony of the bells with this dead who
 returns diffidently
In dream to a home romantically enlarged by dream-
 ing . . . .
Rooms sheathed in walnut . . . halls singular with
 shadow . . .

Where the dreamer walks certain of destination, lighting
Her rapid journey with bobbing candle through rooms and
 stairs
Brought into night-dark being by that light, reflecting now
The panel shine of a closed alcove bed where dreams say
Lie those two so long past dreaming, now sleeping as they
 rested
In that time behind a closed green-painted door
Where a child might tiptoe not disturbing the fluid slumber
 of old age.

There lies in the mind as that dream lay in sleep, the jewel
 of the beginnings,
That which is ancestral, curtained by the catalpa, the high
 swell of the locust,
And the tune of the circling bells. Rejoice it shall never be
 lost,
For losing it life would be a faint thing shuddering vainly in
 the day.

1941

Tomorrow Is A Birthday

Eighty years ago a woman passed
Heavily from shelf to table.   Winter
Was thick on the land.   Through the small glass
Snow glanced at her distorted curve.
Eighty years ago pain swerved her
Foreboding the night at hand.   This I know.
This is not a figure flowing up through fable.
This birth happened as I tell it now.

And as all birth, this was a beginning
And an ending.   She who was lightened
Of that guerdon knew no further rending
And watched few more snows burdening the pines,
Sifting upon the earth.   Eyes I have never seen
Were closed.   A body my memory cannot call back
Reposed.   Yet this has lived with me
That she lived and was dissolved.

From that bearing came vigor drawn from the robust ground
By hard generations, pouring toward age—
Toward eight round decades which would make a life,
The finished sound of them calling for cerement.
Yet the full eight were not tied compactly
But jaggedly rent and again there was an unbinding
And life stopped with difficult secret wailing.

Close to the mind, warm to the nerve,
These decades have turned; interlaced with the past,
Hard and exact with my weight when it enters the circle.
And the circle will haste, and the birthdays will go;
Other decades will form, and again will a body
Be racked.   There will be a dissolving.   Once more bones
That tasted pleasure from this earth will lie down.
The whirl will be marred.   This I know.

1941

The Return

Those the tavern remembered stamped its boards
When coaches groaned over the dust. It was shaken
Then, now more tilted, more unsteady.
Its pictures were of cider and venison—the tall
Words of backwoodsmen poured in whiskey—flight
Of pigeons through walnut twilight.

The churchyard knew only the names within its acre
And there were no graves of their race to call them. They read
The ancient numbers—Cawthorne—Fisher—neighbors
Who died while they were thoughtless of their deathbeds.
Now they would wish them upright again to speak
A word to those who seek.

Did the mill know them? It spoke their tongue of bees,
Cattails and water. It had been given over
To children then and was fresh for secret planning.
Wasps walked the panes. All infancy
Had rested here. Was this the end of yearning,
A timeless spot returning?

Today that house held lisping indolence—
A bleached last son bearing her kindly name.
He strove to find accurate echoes of her
Only to end in his own music. And although
Her reticent belongings cried to the children *pause
Remember with us,*

Yet they could not stay but closed the door
On darkness and mahogany. Oh, go!
This is the past. Nothing is left beside
The voice of summer in the mill. Turn
From this lost hillroad blinded in bees and clover
That today streams over.

1942

Revisit I
Peace at Midnight

In those years above a rooftop,
Serenely shingled, raftered in safety,
Stars locked in their harmonious patterns;
A breeze drove gently from the lake.
Fettered evil exploded never
Over those houses exact in the darkness
Where wrapped in comfort the sleeper lay.
That bed was angeled, that roof strong.

But through those nights the room was beleaguered,
Armies of horror moved in the shadow.
Heads subtly built of sunless hours
And arctic terror reared in corners.
Silent paws ripped at the rug
Clawing the quilt. The young sleeper moved
Followed by nightmare—the faceless vision
Seen in a moonray over the shoulder.

Who shall certify peace at midnight?
What hand make sterile the seeds of violence
While blindness inhabits the soul primitive
Drawn through dream from glacial beginnings?
Will the vast of tomorrow erase this image?
Some day will the mind no longer trouble
When the curtain of skin before the entrance
Shudders at twilight with more than wind?

1942

Revisit IV
Words on Departure

The road which years should have rolled to a stiff chain
Rushed over by gasoline ends in dead flowers
And unrented homes. They blew that iridescent
Bubble too full when their hearts were new
Leaving idleness and black weeds pressing apart
Old machinery of hope. We of the forties
Remark sadly on their contentions. The rubble
Which was once the hotel is a gash in the heart.

Even the wind, that fond enemy, has ripped safety
From the harbor wall. There is dreadful space
In the minute pines which once encircled eternity.
The green chill of the lake pours into sunlight.
These mills are blind—these wharves unpeopled. Speed
Familiar to the time slides through the town
And is gone. The loud word still explores silence
But echo has deserted to the canyons of deed.

What shall happen when the wide city of youth
Lies hollow? When progress, our definition of cheer,
Dies alone? The plan of the past holds no kindness
For now. There will be weeping tomorrow.
This is a farewell to belief—a fear of the goal.
Let the boat, that brave unit of culture, widen
The space from the broken harbor. No wave strangling
Could raise such crest of sorrow in the soul.

1942

Transcontinental

The name Skull Rock sounds as a gong
Among small cedars and the yellow flare
Of quick water.   Yet it will die in the shiver
Of the Diamond A saloon.   Plumb and square
Make space for the stink of fat.   Night and noon
Wives of doctors, clerks and lawyers step
The mud in woman gowns.   Rinse the song
From Skull Rock with the sloshing of their washing.

Grasses and the blossom of Easter will hear no more
The thundering roar of the wilderness.   The words
Of the trapper will go.   The Indian speech
Will be lost like snow.   Springs a new greed
Of beer and rye, steak and coffee—chop house
Open day and night.   Come and buy land,
Stock and wheat land.   Thompson knows about
Land values.   We'll supply every need.

Down from the rimrock those who were the old lovers
Of the land step soberly to the memorial of tragedy.
Into this valley swept the pestilence.   Here
On this blank rock the young warriors were sacrificed
To the morose gods.   Their deaths have not
Been forgotten.   Today their children mourn
Remembering their fathers dead of the pestilence,
And the young men whose bodies were broken.

But this is Town and in its squares no lot
For sorrow.   Banish old tears and ceremony.
Finish the wheels, figure the deals, flash
The loud axes, hurry the taxes, chisel a pavestone.
A day is near when we shall want men
Whose virtue does not rise above roof tops,
Whose thoughts will be churches and rules, ditches and wheat,
Assessments and schools.   Carve on a gravestone.

The solitary of the mountain stares and is gone. The wolf
Looks down in the star-alive night, his hunting ground shifts
To a place of fright black with strange smells.
The trapper returns with his pack from the cedar-clothed land
Where the paint pots bubble. Here is a new hot spring
A troubling well of living. Sage has died
For road. Tin shines in the blue. There
Is nothing here now for anyone but man.

The iron creeps, hammer and spike in a clanging
Song. The end of this building won't be long.
How shall we sing of Skull Rock on that Monday,
That day of best grade lumber west of Chi?
Ragged stock upon the range that
The wolf has left forever. Though this stagger
The heart—a blunder of loss with nothing for gain—
Shall we sing it as change, as the morning of wonder?

1946

Dorchester Plate

Bound with blue where thirteen stars
space demurely, crowned by an eagle,
flecked with marionettes under stiff trees,
the past climbs to an easy hill.

When could years have shown thus—
glazed—circular? Yet grandfathers of living
women darkened this grass with death,
sweated through that voiceless mill.

So soon does blood shrink to
the dimensions of a shelf. The gaudy tones
of passion spill at last on
this cycle of pottery—this mirror of the unreal.

1946

Language Of Pain

This is our ancestral war, twisted
Clear and rosy through our web of living,
Dear to the nerves,
Savory with the lore
of granduncles, parades.

Saplings set the morning Lincoln died
Retain that sanctity and pride to the
Last orchard branch.
The birthday of the old
Is bright with Gettysburg.

Today gigantic strides us weak.
Its mechanic roar is not the tongue
By which we speak
Of fraticide, disorder
And the fame of war.

So the translated agony of dream
Visits one in proud rooms where the sleeper yearns,
Parting dark folds,
To watch the hesitant poplar
Trembling like youth bereaved;

While a tune commonplace with years
Once more calls tears to one who loves in shadow
The bearded bluecoat,
Tenting and sad for peace,
Within a graceless world.

1946

Over Patras

Galaxies flee forever from each other.
Their floor today is plotted by the wise.
Orion has discharged his mysteries,
Feared by those watchers at the Lion Gate
Who saw planet and constellation roar
Over the far and terrible sanctuary.
Men have dared knowledge, so the sky today
Unfolds for them with pendulum clarity.

But I am ignorant.   For me the Chair
Hangs in the sky clear and provocative.
My mind cares nothing for these certitudes.
My truths are older, so I peer and crouch,
With stare as shaken as the Mycenean,
Seeing the comet flaring over Patras.

1959

Ahsahta Press

Series Editors: Orvis C. Burmaster
                 James H. Maguire
                 A. Thomas Trusky

Fall, 1975: **The Selected Poems of Norman Macleod**
Introduction by A. Thomas Trusky
ISBN 0-916272-00-1

Spring, 1976: **Gwendolen Haste, Selected Poems**
Preface by Carol Mullaney
ISBN 0-916272-01-X

Summer, 1976: **Peggy Pond Church, New and Selected Poems**
Introduction by T. M. Pearce
ISBN 0-916272-02-8

Winter, 1976: **Poems,** Marnie Walsh

Ahsahta Press volumes are published by the Boise State University Department of English and printed and bound by the BSU Printing and Graphics Center. Price: $2 per volume.

Mail orders: University Campus Store, Boise State University, 1910 College Boulevard, Boise, Idaho 83725.